Preparing for the Storm

Bible Study

In the summer of 2004, our son, Cliff at the age of 24, was diagnosed with terminal cancer. As we walked through the next seven years, I could see how God had prepared Cliff to face a storm above all others. The purpose of this study is to see from God's Word how we can prepare to face the storms in our lives with courage and confidence of victory.

Terri Lee Jenkin

Dedication

Dedicated to my son, Cliff, who entered heaven on April 1, 2011 leaving a testimony to the Goodness and Loving Kindness of God.

Dedicated to Bill, my husband and favorite preacher, who has taught me and challenged me from God's Word. Together we walk hand in hand facing each storm with courage and confidence in God and our Savior Jesus Christ.

Contents

For consistency, quotations are taken from the King James Version of the Bible

Lesson One: Approaching Storms

In the physical world there are snow storms, rain storms, hail storms, tornados, hurricanes, floods, and earthquakes. At times we can see a storm developing, and its arrival is not a surprise. Others come upon us suddenly with no warning, catching us off guard. The amount of damage caused by storms varies in degree, but it is not the damage I want to focus on in this study. My focus is not on the why or the purpose of the storm. These questions will answer themselves if you have prepared for the storm...they will be answered through your preparation.

We lived in Florida for nearly 20 years and know pretty well what is necessary to prepare for hurricane season. Preparing early relieves the anxiety and stress when the storm is upon you.

Our initial exposure to a hurricane happened during our first church plant in Beverly Hills, Florida. It was Labor Day weekend and Hurricane Elena was stalled in the Gulf of Mexico, 50 miles off the coast threatening us for three days. Preparations were made, and we were ready. At the last minute, she headed north toward the Panhandle of Florida and eventually went onshore near Biloxi, Mississippi.

Storms in our life do not always happen that way. More often than not, we do not have prior knowledge of their arrival nor do they "head north" at the last minute.

Each spring, a number of tornadoes hit the United States. Several times, there is devastation in areas that had never experienced such a storm. Testimony from victims state they never expected a tornado to ever hit their area.
I may not be able to tell you when, but I can tell you according to the Word of God, the storms are coming.

Throughout Scripture, God's sovereignty and man's human responsibility are shown walking hand in hand. We may not be able to comprehend it, but that doesn't make it any less true.

Knowing God has chosen us in Him before the foundation of the world for a purpose; that *we should be holy and without blame before Him in love (Ephesians 1:4),* we can go forward with great confidence that whatever storm we encounter, He has purposely set it before us so we might be *conformed to the image of his Son* (Jesus Christ) *(Romans 8:29).*

1. *2 Corinthians 4:17*
   What does Paul call our afflictions?

   How long do they last?

   What do they result in?

2. Although there is a human responsibility in preparing for the storms ahead, without God you are bound to fail. *Philippians 4:13* tells you through Christ _____.

Philippians 4:19 God will _____
"according to his riches in glory by Christ Jesus".

During his battle with cancer our son, Cliff, wrote the following:

In the days when ships sailed the seas powered by nothing but the winds in their sails, the oceans were the great highways of the world. On the waves fortunes were made and lost, honor obtained, lives were built but also taken away. Some men went to sea because they had no other choice, no other way to make a living. Some went to quench a thirst for adventure, some to become rich. Some went with years of experience as able seamen, some as new hands, some as seasoned officers, and some as mere schoolboys learning a trade. But all who went understood that no matter who they were or where they came from, the sea would demand respect. The sea treats all men equally--rich or poor, old or young, experienced or not; the sea knows not nor cares. Some went upon the waters with enormous ships that would carry hundreds of men and tons of cargo and equipment. Some traveled in light vessels with scant provisions. But the sea was always the sea: It would roar and foam, spraying ship and crew with volumes of rushing water; it would blow and rage, ripping masts and sails from their places; it would lie calm and serene, coaxing songs and dreams from delighted travelers. The only thing anyone could know for sure about an upcoming voyage was that he would be sure to experience both calm and storms.

Life is like a voyage on the sea. We embark with goals in mind and provisions in hand. Some have a firmer idea of what lies in store than others. Some have much more experience, some have more advantages. But all can be sure of one thing; trials will come, as surely as the periods of calm and peace.

When a captain would prepare for a voyage, he would first make sure he had the proper maps and charts. He would check his compass and his instruments to see that they were true. But not only before he left--while at sea he would constantly be looking over his charts, verifying his location, marking his progress, making note of any possible dangers ahead. If he were entering unknown waters he would talk with other men who had sailed there before and ask their advice. He would constantly watch the winds and waves for signs of impending storms.

In the same way we ought not to embark on our journey without the proper guidance. We must constantly look to Scripture as the chart which marks our path. We must use the Holy Spirit as a compass to assure us that we are pointed in the right direction. We must seek counsel in prayer as we face unknown situations. Just as no captain would attempt to steer a course using merely his instincts and innate sense of direction, we must not rely solely on our own wisdom in order to guide our steps aright.

When a captain would approach a coast, or a harbor, or some area with dangerous currents or underwater obstacles, he would slow his ship and take aboard a pilot. The pilot was an expert mariner; one who would have had great experience with the specific waters in which he sailed. The pilot would know the area far better than could be seen on any chart or map, and thus would be prepared for whatever difficulties that may arise. A captain, normally the sole authority over every aspect of his ship, would relinquish all his power to the pilot. It was the pilot who would command, who would order the men to their tasks, who would direct the helmsman, who would call for sails to be reefed or furled. To insure the safety of the ship and the entire voyage, a captain was required to place complete confidence in the pilot; and he would do so, because he understood the superiority of the pilot's knowledge and experience.

Only with divine assistance can we hope to maneuver the oceans of life, completing our voyage in success and honor. Only through the power of God in our lives can we safely sail to heaven's shore.

In the same way we must give place in our lives to the commanding presence of our Savior Jesus Christ. We cannot afford to think that we know better than He what actions to take or what paths to pursue. As we make decisions we must always bear in mind that our Heavenly Pilot knows far better than we what we ought to do. In our lives trials will come. We will find ourselves approaching rocks and shoals, or caught in dangerous currents, and we will despair of what to do. We must remember that Jesus is our Pilot. He knows how to take us safely through the dangers to the calm waters of the harbor. We must depend on Him, and trust Him to pilot us.

Prepare now, be ready: Storms are inevitable.

God desires to use these storms to draw us closer to Him and bring glory to Himself, but Satan wants to take the same storms and cause us to be ineffective and defeated.

3. Write out *1 Peter 5:8-11* in your own words.

Challenge:

With a hurricane approaching, a store manager stated "The flow of customers is pretty steady, but everyone waits until the worst of the storm to start preparing."

Plan to be committed to this study so you are not the one waiting until the worst of the storm to start preparing.

Lesson Two: Building on a Firm Foundation

We have all seen pictures of communities devastated by a storm. Often homes are destroyed because of poor construction and having no foundation. The foundation of a building and what that foundation is built upon can determine how well it endures a storm.

When building a home, there are typically three types of foundations. Depending on where you build, you might have a basement, crawl space, or slab. Regardless of what type of foundation the house has, that foundation includes footings which go deep into the earth.

1. Who is the ONE foundation whose footing is sure?
   1 Corinthians 3:11

It is important to realize you MUST be anchored to this foundation.

2. What instructions are given in order to be anchored to this foundation?
   Acts 16:31

   John 1:12

   To receive = to take action on your belief:
   Matt 7:24-27

3. What do you need to understand in order to believe?
   Romans 3:23 says you are a _____.

   Romans 6:23 Tells you the payment for your sin is _____.

Isaiah 59:2 Your sin has _____ you from God.

Ephesians 2:8, 9 There is _____ you can do to provide that payment;

BUT

Romans 5:8 Christ _____ for you;

1 Peter 3:18; John 14:6 That He might

_____

The Bible tells us there is an action you need to take:
Acts 3:19 "_____ ye therefore, and be converted, that your sins may be blotted out. . ."

Acts 26:20 "... that they should _____ and _____, and do works meet for repentance."

Works meet for repentance does not mean to work for your salvation, but after you are saved; your works are evidence of your turning from sin to God.

"If you confess with your mouth the Lord Jesus and believe in your heart that God has raised Him from the dead, you will be saved" (Romans 10:9).

4. Has there been a time in your life when you received Jesus Christ as your personal Savior?
(Write out your testimony here)

5. If there has never been a time in your life when you made the decision to accept Jesus Christ as your Savior, **Take Action TODAY**

>*Hebrews 3:15 "_____if ye will hear his voice, harden not your hearts".*

>*2 Corinthians 6:2 "_____ is the time to accept Jesus as Savior; Behold, _____ is the accepted time; behold, _____ is the day of salvation"*

You can pray this simple prayer right where you are:
Lord, I know I am a sinner, I know I cannot save myself, I know that Jesus died for MY sins...I am repenting of my sins and receiving Jesus Christ as MY Savior.

>If you have taken this action; **Praise the Lord! (share your decision with others.)**

You are not simply involved in a religion; you are now involved in a RELATIONSHIP.

6. When you receive Him, what have you become?
>*John 1:12*

This relationship demands personal attention. Christ is not just our Savior, but also Lord, and He commands obedience.

7. What comparison does the following verse make to obeying God's Word and disobeying God's Word?
>*Luke 6:46-49*

True salvation results in a changed life

8. What do these verses say about this new life?
    2 Corinthians 5:17

    Galatians 2:20

9. Christ cannot simply be a part of your life; He must be the center of your life.
    Exodus 20:5-6; Exodus 34:14 "God is a
    _____ *God;"*

    Matthew 6:24 "You cannot serve
    _____ *." * This can be translated money or wealth.

    Why?

Because of who God is, you must make a decision regarding your loyalty toward Him:

10. The choice is yours.
    Joshua 24:15 "And if it seem evil unto you to serve the Lord, _____ *you this day whom ye will serve; whether the gods which your fathers served that were on the other side of the flood, or the gods of the Amorites, in whose land ye dwell: but as for me and my house, we will serve The Lord."*

Challenge:
What changes in your life are necessary to allow Jesus Christ to have priority in your daily walk?

Lesson Three: Relying on the Water of the Word

I was recently listening to the weather channel when they gave instructions for preparing for a hurricane. The top priority on the list of supplies was water. I remember the first hurricane we were subject to after moving to Florida. We filled every available container as well as the bathtub and washing machine. When or if the hurricane hit, we would have water to sustain us through the storm.

The Water of the Word must be stored up in your heart so when the storm is upon you, you have what is necessary to sustain you.   When we began our journey with Cliff's cancer, we lived in the medical center for six weeks. Four of those weeks were spent in ICU not knowing whether our son would live or die. Scripture that was stored away in our hearts began to rush to the surface, nourishing us through the worst of times.

God's Word will better equip you to face anything that comes your way.

1. *John 17:17* The Word of God is _____

Truth is fact, a certainty, that which is absolutely reliable, constant, totally secure. TRUTH CANNOT CHANGE! A person's perspective does NOT change the truth.

2. Knowing the Word of God is truth, how can that affect you as you face each day?

15

3. What does 2 *Timothy 3:16* tell us about God's Word?

> *"All scripture is given by* _____
> *of God. . .*
>
> *And is profitable*
>
> *for* _____ (what you
> believe)
>
> *for* _____ (literally means to drag
> to the light)
>
> *for* _____ (to bring back to where you
> ought to be)
>
> *for* _____ *in righteousness"*
> (keeps you going in the right way)

Inspiration refers to the way God made his truth known. The word appears only once in the New Testament and literally means God breathed. With all of His energy God 'blew' His very words into the writers of Scripture, while still allowing for the writers' personalities and styles to come through.

Scripture comes directly from the mouth of God. It is accurate, authoritative and admonitory. It shows you where you have gone wrong, how to get right and how to keep going right.

4. For what purpose is Scripture given?
   2 Timothy 3:17

5. The Word of God is necessary for what?
Romans 10:14

Romans 10:17

6. According to these verses, what does the Word of God gives you?
Psalms 119:129-130

Psalms 119:104

Psalms 119:105

The Word of God will affect your thinking, your confidence, and your choices.

7. List some verses that have helped you specifically during difficult days:

8. How does knowing these verses help you to be prepared for the storms that lie ahead?

Challenge:
Your growth depends on being in the Word of God.
Develop a plan for getting into the Word of God on a daily basis.

Lesson Four: Getting to Know God

The Word of God gives us understanding of who God is and who we are to God: *"For I know the thoughts that I think toward you, saith the LORD, thoughts of peace, and not of evil, to give you an expected end" (Jeremiah 29:11).*

Know: The Character of God
1. What do these verses tell you regarding the character of God?

Genesis 28:3

Genesis 15:1

Genesis 22:8

Exodus 15:26

Psalms 18:46

Luke 1:37

Revelations 19:11

2. What do these verses say about the character of Jesus Christ?

John 10:30

Hebrews 13:8

3. What does this verse tell you about the character of the Holy Spirit?

John 14:16, 17

Know: The Power of God
4. How powerful is your God?
Jeremiah 32:17

Ephesians 1:19-20

The first word power in Ephesians 1:19 speaks of a raw power, the ability to do wonders, and overcome any resistance. Add *"exceeding greatness"* and it describes a power that goes far beyond what you might ask or think.

The phase *"us-ward who believe"* tells you this power is directed toward you personally because of your salvation. There is no problem so insurmountable it cannot be solved by God.

The second word power speaks of strength and physical ability. When you add the phases *"the working"* and *"mighty"* it describes a power in action showing God's strength in my life and God's strength in your life.

You may not know what storms are on the horizon, but one you recognize that God IS all-powerful, you can know there is no storm He cannot calm.

5. What do these verses say about God's power?
Romans 13:1

Ephesians 3:20

Jude 1:25

6. How can knowing God's power prepare you for the storms ahead?
Ephesians 6:10

Know: God is Faithful
7. How does His faithfulness relate to the storms you might face?
Lamentations 3:22-23

Understanding who God is and how that relates to you as His child will give you the confidence to move forward facing each day as it comes with courage.

Challenge:
Determine to find out who God is through the Word of God.

Lesson Five: Getting to Know God More

During the seven years our son, Cliff, walked through his journey with terminal cancer, his greatest desire was that his students and all those who heard his story would have a clear understanding of God's loving kindness.

Five years ago today I woke up from a surgery in which my adrenal glands were removed. For the first time in weeks I was lucid enough to really understand what was going on around me. During the preceding weeks I had become dimly aware of the cancer the doctors had discovered in my liver, but the constant surge of adrenaline had kept me from being truly mentally alert. Now it was time to face the facts. I could barely move my arms, I didn't have enough strength to sit up or change position in bed, and the muscles in my legs were completely atrophied. The cancer had spread through my liver to such an extent that the doctors were thinking of my lifespan in terms of months. And to add insult to injury (though this was not evident until many weeks later when I could actually stand), I was six inches shorter because of compression fractures in my spine.

[Through physical therapy and time, Cliff regained his strength and went back to teaching]

Time passes. In many ways my new life is like my old one, and in many ways it is very different. In the past five years I have gotten married, finished a master's degree, traveled to 14 countries on 3 continents, taught hundreds of teenagers, become a volleyball coach and gotten married (No, I didn't get married twice, but I figured it was worth throwing in there again. I mean, really...I got married!) God has showered me with blessings over the last 5 years. The list above is just the major ones. I could go on and on with "little" blessings that wouldn't really sound like a big deal to anyone else. I don't still need a cane. I can stand and pivot and take steps without worrying about falling. I can go up and down steps. I sleep through the night. I've learned many things in the past five years . . . I learned what it feels like to be 80 years old. . . I learned what it feels like to be very sick. . . I learned that most people don't mind my hunched back.

But the real treasure, amid all the blessings and all the lessons of my new life, has been what I have learned about who God is. Now when I read a Psalm 103, it MEANS something to me that it wouldn't have (I don't say couldn't have) before. I know that God really does treat His people with that kind of tenderness. When I read about the trying of our faith resulting in patience, I understand. When I read about faith in unseen things, I get it. I'm not saying I've got the whole Bible figured out. God is infinite, and naturally as we learn more about Him we also learn more about how much we don't know. But God has arranged these lessons for me; to conform me to the image of His Son. Cancer is part of that curriculum for me. And I wouldn't trade these five years for anything.

Know: God is Loving and Kind
It is important to recognize, understand and believe that your God is loving and kind.

1. List His benefits according to *Psalm 103:2-5*
Bless the LORD, O my soul, and forget not all his benefits:

There are numerous books written to answer the age old question, "how can a loving God allow so much pain?" When you have an understanding of God's loving kindness before storms overtake you, the question "how" fades into the background.

Know: God is Wise
2. In His wisdom, what has God has shown us?
Ephesians 1:7-9

3. Why is Wisdom more precious than anything else you can desire?
Proverbs 3:13-15

Proverbs 2:10, 20

4. How can knowing that God is wise and that He never makes mistakes help you to prepare for the storms ahead?

Know: God is a Sovereign God
5. What did Job recognize even though he did not see the future or could not understand God's plan?
Job 23:10

6. What is God doing in your life, even when you cannot see?
Romans 8:28-30

Philippians 2:13

Romans 9:20, 21

Ephesians 2:10 says we are *"God's workmanship created _____."*

God's workmanship: a work of art; a masterpiece. When God wants to express himself, He does so through His children.

For many years I read *Ephesians 2:10* and limited it to believing that as I walked along in this Christian life, God had some GOOD WORKS -- ministry opportunities, witnessing opportunities -- for me to do. He desires to exhibit Christ through good works.

But then the storms began to form, and I was challenged to take a closer look at good works. "Good" has a wide range of meanings: benevolent, profitable, useful, beneficial, excellent, virtuous and suitable. So, I came to the realization - anything in my life that would be beneficial, profitable, and useful to God would be considered good.

We should not call bad what God calls good!

7. How does *Psalms 84:11* relate to the storms that come upon you?

8. What do these verses say about equipping you?
   2 Timothy 2:19-21; 2 Timothy 3:16-17

9. How will knowing God is in control prepare you for the storms ahead?

Challenge:
View everything in your life from the hand of God and as good.

Lesson Six: Recognizing the Holy Spirit

The Holy Spirit is the third person of the Godhead. It is important to understand what part He has in your life, and how He affects your everyday walk as a child of God as you prepare for the storms.

1. *Acts 5:3, 4* God and the Holy Spirit are _____

2. He possesses all the attributes of deity
      1 Corinthians 2:11-12 _____

      Psalms 139:7 _____

      Job 33:4 _____

      1 John 5:6 _____

The Holy Spirit is Personal
3. When you accept Jesus Christ as your Savior, what does the Holy Spirit of God do?
      Romans 8:9

      1 Corinthians 6:19

      John 14:16-17

4. What does that make you?
      1 Corinthians 3:16;   2 Corinthians 6:16

5. What do these verses tell us about the Holy Spirit?
      Romans 8:9-11

      2 Corinthians 1:22; Ephesians 1:13

My husband has a sermon titled "Navigating through the Unknown" from Joshua 3 which includes three truths: **God's unfailing promises, God's unfailing power, and God's guidance through the unknown.** God told Joshua; *"As I was with Moses, so I will be with you" (Joshua 1:5; 3:7).* That same God who was with Moses and who was with Joshua is with each believer in the form of the Holy Spirit.

Sometimes, the fear of the unknown can cripple you. In 1985, God called our family to Florida to plant churches. We bought a book to familiarize us with the state, and what we found did not thrill our children. It was the lightening capital of the U.S., hurricanes were common, fire ants roamed the ground and alligators occupied the ponds; all unknown things to us. Yet God, though the ministry of the Holy Spirit relieved those fears and led us there to minister for 20 years.

The Holy Spirit's Purpose
6. What do the following verses tell you about the Holy Spirit's purpose?
John 14:26

John 16:13

Romans 8:14

1 Corinthians 2:9-16

7. How can we go forward with confidence?
John 14:16-18

When God speaks of *"another"*, He is speaking of one identical in nature. A difference between the Lord Jesus and the Holy Spirit is Jesus ministered from without; the Holy Spirit ministers from within.

Jesus calls the Holy Spirit *"another"* comforter; one exactly like Himself to encourage and meet your spiritual needs.

The Holy Spirit takes the Word of God and makes it alive and applicable to your life. He illumines spiritual truth so you can see and understand God's purpose written in His Word. Simply stated: The Holy Spirit puts the pieces together for you.

In the springtime, flooding takes place in many areas of the country. In preparation, sandbags are piled to keep out the water. I liken those sandbags to the Spirit of God. He enables you to pile truths up where they will be most effective in protecting your mind so you can be prepared for the flooding of doubt and discouragement that comes with a storm.

Our responsibility to the Holy Spirit
8. What is your responsibility in regard to the Holy Spirit?
   Ephesians 5:1

9. What are the two warnings given you?
   Ephesians 4:30

   1 Thessalonians 5:19

The warning in Ephesians means to make sad or bring pain to the Spirit of God. The warning in 1 Thessalonians means to hinder or resist the Holy Spirit's guidance in your life.

10. *Ephesian 4:30-31* gives some ways in which you can grieve the Holy Spirit. What are they?

You should not extinguish the influences of the Holy Spirit in your hearts. The result of quenching the Holy Spirit is you living in a state of darkness with no understanding of how God is working in your life. Quench the Holy Spirit and the "electricity" will go out before the storm.

11. How does the Holy Spirit assure you that God is always with you and will never leave you?
    John 14:16

12. Using two columns, list the evidences of being *Spirit Filled* from Ephesians and the evidences of *letting the Word of Christ dwell in you richly* from Colossians.

Being Spirit Filled	Let the Word of Christ Dwell in you
Ephesians 5:18-6:6	*Colossians 3:16-4:5*

13. What is your conclusion?

Challenge: Make the decision to be in God's Word, and allow the Holy Spirit to have free reign in your life.

Lesson Seven: Applying God's Armor

1. Write *James 1:2* in your own words.

When a conquering army returned after being victorious in battle, the people would line the streets proclaiming "Count it all joy" which can be interpreted as "Hail, welcome". That is what God wants you to do when you face trials.

Satan wants to use the storms in your life to destroy you; God wants to use the same storms to make you stronger . . . the choice is yours.

My son-in-law is an officer in the United States Army. When he was in Iraq, he did not go out without putting on the proper armor and weapons fully prepared to meet the enemy. God has given Christians armor and weapons too.

2. What does *Ephesians 6:12* tell you about the battle you are fighting?

Put On
Put on is the act of clothing yourself. God instructs you to put on the whole (ALL) armor for your own benefit and to never take it off.
3. Why must you put on the armor?
    Ephesians 6:11, 13

The armor is to be put on at the time of your salvation and kept on for the duration of the conflict, not only when you are in the midst of a storm.

4. What qualities and characteristics are you to put on?

Galatians 3:27 "For as many of you as have been baptized into Christ have put on _____."

Romans 13:14 "But put ye on _____ and make not provision for the flesh, to fulfil the lusts thereof."

Colossians 3:12 "Put on therefore, as the elect of God, _____ "

Ephesians 4:24 "And that ye put on the new man, which after God is created in _____ and true _____."

These characteristics and qualities are to become a part of your very nature.

The Armor of God

Ephesians 6:14-17
Girdle of _____ – Both the truth of God's Word and your personal truthfulness, honesty and candor are the foundation of your life.

Breastplate of _____ – You have the imputed righteousness of Christ, which produces right conduct and holy living. It protects important areas including your testimony, confidence of salvation and eternal life.

Feet shod with the preparation of the Gospel of _____ – You are ready to do whatever is needed because you have peace with God (judicial) and the peace of God (experiential). You are to go forward with a peace of mind and heart that the world can never understand.

Shield of _____ – Your faith in Christ and His Word will protect you from the temptations that Satan shoots at you constantly.

Helmet of _____ – Your salvation protects you from Satan's attacks on the mind, such as doubt concerning security and assurance of salvation, discouragement in your living and service, and every possible intellectual attack (i.e. evolution, secular psychology).

Sword of the _____ – The Word of God is the only offensive weapon. The Christian needs to be skilled in using it to face all attacks of untruth.

5. What might cause you not to put the whole armor on?

Our Arsenal
In addition to the armor, you have much more in your arsenal. It is important that you recognize your spiritual resources: spiritual resources which are available to each one who has received Jesus Christ as Savior and now has the Holy Spirit dwelling in him/her.

6. According to these verses, what spiritual resources are available to you?
    1 Corinthians 1:30

    Ephesians 1:7

    Ephesians 1:8

31

Hebrews 4:16

Romans 5:5

Grace is giving to you what you do not deserve.
Mercy is holding back from you what you do deserve.

You needed your sin to be paid for and Christ did that on the cross of Calvary.

7. When sin comes knocking at your door, you DO NOT have to answer.
However, if you do sin, what is available to you?
1 John 1:9

Challenge:
As you walk through this day and the days ahead, recognize God has given you, through Christ, everything you need to live victorious as you face trials and temptations.

Lesson Eight: Claiming the Promises of God

God's Word is Truth. The Word tells you He has equipped
you to face any storm that might rage against you.
God is constant and faithful in keeping His promises, and
therefore is worthy of your trust.

What God says He will do, He will do.

God's "promise" is an assurance, a pledge, a guarantee given
for your good and on which you are totally dependent on
Him for. It is in His power to give as he pleases; a favor
which you can obtain ONLY from Him, and not by any self-
determining effort of your own.

The Jewish people were characterized in a very specific
manner by the promises they received from God: the
promises given to Abraham, Isaac, Jacob, Moses, and the
prophets. God promised to be their God: to protect, support,
and save them; to give them the Promised Land and
ultimately to give them the Messiah.

*1. Write in your own words the promises given to the
Israelites:*

> *Deuteronomy 33:25*

> *Isaiah 40:31*

> *Psalms 50:15*

> *Jeremiah 29:12*

> *Psalms 91:15*

> *Genesis 28:15*

Deuteronomy 33:27

Joshua 1:9

Psalms 27:1

Psalms 138:7-8

Psalms 46:1-11

Although the preceding promises were given specifically to the Israelites, you can make application because God's promises extend to you through the blood of Christ.

None of God's promises failed: the promise of grace and mercy, the pardon of sin, the sanctifying of His people, support during temptation and trials, guidance in uncertainty, peace in death and eternal life. All of these were fulfilled through His promise to send Jesus Christ into the world.

The great promise of the Old Testament was the promise of the coming Messiah.
"And I will put enmity between thee and the woman, and between thy seed and her seed; it shall bruise thy head, and thou shalt bruise his heel" (Genesis 3:15).

2. Who is the seed?
   Genesis 17:7 and Galatians 3:16.

3. According to the following verses who is the great promise of the New Testament?
   Acts 2:33; Luke 11:13; Luke 24:49

4. At the time of salvation, a believer is promised the presence of the Holy Spirit as helper, tutor and guide.

How long does the presence of the Holy Spirit last?
   John 14:16

5. What does *2 Corinthians 1:20-22* tell you about the promises of God?

6. In *2 Peter 1:3-4*, Peter submits to the Gentiles that God had also given them promises. What are some of them?

It was of considerable importance to the comfort of the Gentiles that these promises were made to them, and that salvation was not exclusively for the Jews.

7. Because of your relationship with Christ, you can claim these promises.
   John 14:13

   Colossians 2:10

   Romans 8:37-39

   1 John 4:4

   1 John 5:4-5

   1 Corinthians 15:57

   Romans 8:31

   Philippians 1:6

Philippians 4:7

Hebrews 13:5

Matthew 7:7-8

John 6:35

8. It is important to note while the promises of God are afforded to all believers, they do carry stipulations. What stipulation did God give the Israelites in *2 Chronicles 7:14*?

9. In *John 15:4-10,* what is the stipulation given to believers?

10. While receiving the promises of God is not by any self-determining effort of your own, the fulfillment of His promises IS directly related to obedient responses of God's children.

> *Lamentations 3:22-25 "It is of the Lord's mercies that we are not consumed, because his compassions fail not. They are new every morning: great is thy faithfulness. The LORD is my portion, saith my soul; therefore will I hope in him. The LORD is good unto them _____ _____ for him, to the soul that _____ him."*

As I faced the storm of our son's cancer, I found two great promises to be my anchor:
- *"For the LORD God is a sun and shield: the LORD will give grace and glory: no good thing will He withhold from them that walk uprightly" (Psalms 84:11).*

- *"Thou wilt keep him in perfect peace, whose mind is stayed on thee: because he trusteth in thee" (Isaiah 26:3).*

11. If God says there is; *"no good thing will he withhold from them that walk uprightly"* - then how should you view the storms in your life?

12. The *"him"* and *"he"* in *Isaiah 26:3* refer to the believer in Jesus Christ. In what ways can you keep your mind stayed on Jesus Christ?

**As you prepare for the storms ahead
KNOW there is GREAT HOPE in the promises of God!**

Challenge:
Humble yourself, seek His face, and turn from any sin that would hinder God's fulfillment of His promises in your life.

Lesson Nine: Standing on Praying Ground

Prayer is the power that needs to be installed in every life. Power that never goes out. God wants you to be hooked up and connected 24/7. God does not want your prayer life to be a backup generator; flipped on only during a storm.

1. What would cause you to become disconnected?
    Psalms 66:17-20

    Isaiah 59:2

2. What does *Psalms 34:15 and Proverbs 15:29* tell you about God hearing?

3. *John 9:31* tells you God does not have to hear _____ but God hears _____.

4. What do these verses say about prayer?
    1 Peter 4:7

    Colossians 4:2

    Luke 18:1

    Philippians 4:6

    Ephesians 6:18

5. What do these verses say about commitment to prayer?
    Psalm 102:2 "Hide not thy face from me in the day
    when I am in trouble; _____: in
    the day when I call answer me speedily."

Psalm 88:1-2 "O LORD God of my salvation, I have
_____ *before thee: Let*
my prayer come before thee: _____
unto my cry."

Nehemiah 1:6 "Let thine ear now be _____,
and thine eyes open, that thou _____
of thy servant."

Prayer is blessed fellowship.

Prayer keeps us in the presence of God and by living constantly in His presence, we will reflect His character.

6. What is God's promise to His children who are committed to prayer?

>   *John 14:13-14*

>   *Matthew 6:5-8*

7. What are some conditions for prayer?

>   *1 John 3:22*

>   *1 John 5:14*

>   *Mark 11:24*

God's answer at first may be unclear or different from what you expected or desired, or the answer may be delayed. Sometimes you ask the Lord to do things that are not for your good, the good of others, or the ultimate fulfillment of God's plan.

We see life from a finite viewpoint; God sees the beginning and the end of all things. The Lord alone knows how your prayer requests fit into His purpose, which is for your good.

In 2004 when Cliff, at the age of 24, was diagnosed with cancer, life changed for all of us. I became Cliff's caregiver as he began chemotherapy. I remember sitting day after day in his little apartment pleading with God to heal him and not to let him die. After many days of prayer, God answered with this verse.

> *"When Jesus heard that, he said, This sickness is not unto death, but for the glory of God, that the Son of God might be glorified thereby" (John 11:4).*

God was not telling me Cliff was not going to die. What the Holy Spirit impressed on my heart was: regardless of whether God healed Cliff or not, HE, God, would be glorified. As Cliff walked through the storm for seven years, his faith did indeed glorify God.

> "All of the good that was in him came from God. He was a reflection to us of God. If he was only a reflection though, then how much greater must our Lord be! I know that if Mr. Jenkin wanted anything it would be that his life and death would bring glory to God."
>
> Written by one of Cliff's students

8. What promises are given in these verses regarding prayer?
   Jeremiah 33:3

   Ephesians 3:20

   Galatians 6:6

Jesus gives you an example of praying before the storm.
Think of all Jesus Christ was about to face. One of his
priorities was to pray to His Father.

9. What was the result of Jesus' prayer in Luke *22:42-46?*

Storm after storm will sweep over your way. But being near
Him in utter devotion will keep you plugged in to His power;
power for our everyday tasks and power to keep us sweet
while we are learning life's hardest lessons.

Challenge: Be confident – there will be storms in your life.
Prepare now by keeping the lines of communication open
between you and the Lord.

Lesson Ten: Faithfulness in the Local Church

During the six weeks of Cliff's hospitalization, we sat day after day beside him. Every day someone from his church or from the Christian academy where he taught drove the four hour round trip to see him; sometimes staying for only a few minutes. Cliff's faithfulness to his local church was part of his preparation to face the greatest storm of his life.

In October of 2004, after meeting with the cancer specialist in Florida, Cliff was given the choice to stay in Florida and begin chemo treatments or to go back to New Hampshire and begin his treatments there. Although he was raised in Florida and the church there loved him and could have ministered to him, he chose New Hampshire because that was where his church family was.

The Universal Church
1. Matthew 16:18
> Who builds the church?

> How strong is the church?

2. Acts 20:28
> With whose blood was it purchased?

The Baptism of the Holy Spirit takes place at the time you accept Christ as your Savior. The Holy Spirit comes and lives inside of you placing you into the body of believers with Christ as the head.

3. Paul is comparing the body of Christ to what?
Ephesians 5:30

1 Corinthians 12:12-13

4. Fill in the blank to see what God expects of the church regarding unity.

Romans 12:4-5 "For as we have many members in _____ body, and all members have not the same office: So we, being many, are _____ body in Christ, and every _____ members _____ of another."

Ephesians 4:4 "There is _____ body, and _____ Spirit, even as ye are called in _____ hope of your calling;"

The local church

The book of Acts tells about the beginning of the local church. First & 2 Corinthians, Galatians, Ephesians, Philippians, Colossians, and 1 & 2 Thessalonians were all written to local churches. First & 2 Timothy and Titus were written to pastors of local churches.

5. *Acts 2:41-42*
   Who makes up the local church?

   What should the he activities of the local church be?

6. *Ephesians 4:12*
   What is the he purpose of the local church?

7. *Acts 6:1-4*
   The twelve [vs 6 calls them apostles] had two major responsibilities: What were they?

   Meeting the physical needs of the believers was also important. What do verses 1-4 tell you regarding how they met those needs?

God has equipped the church to minister to one another. Each person within the Body of Christ is important. Each person within the local church is important.

8. Meditate on *Ephesians 4:16.* Write it in your own words.

While my husband and I were ministering in a local church, I met a lady whose husband had passed away. She shared with me how the church family surrounded her with love and support. This is a poem she wrote to express her thankfulness to them.

Sharing
-a poem to our brothers and sisters in Christ

Sharing the concern
Your prayers and visits meant so much
The words of encouragement with a gentle touch
Sharing the concern

Sharing the load
Gifts of food and cash helped us to cope
The hugs and the prayers kept giving us hope
Sharing the load

Sharing the pain
You hurt with us and time you gave freely
To be there for us – your love was shown clearly
Sharing the pain

Sharing the joy
You stood with us as we looked to heaven
Assured that Jim was starting his reunion
Sharing the joy

You have been there to share
Each step of this journey
And while there were times
Nothing could stop the hurting

You were the arms of God
So He could give us an embrace
And we felt Him near
With His amazing grace

"Thank you" seems too easy
"We appreciate it" not enough, and yet
Please know we love you
And will never forget
The Carter Family (used by permission)

8. What instructions is God giving to the believers within the Universal Church as well as believers in the local church?

Ephesians 4:32

Colossians 3:13-16

Romans 13:8

John 13:34

1 Peter 4:10

Galatians 6:2

9. According to *Hebrews 10:24, 25* what instruction is given to you concerning the local church?

When the writer of Hebrews tells the believers to consider one another, to provoke to love and to good works, he wants them to be determined to have unity and strength within the church so they can hold fast to what they had been taught.

God considers the local church an essential part of the Christian's life.

Challenge:
If you are not attending a Bible believing and teaching church, ask God to give you wisdom in finding a local church and then get involved.

Lesson Eleven: Looking toward Heaven

The Bible refers to heaven in three different ways:

The vast expanse of space surrounding the earth referred to as the atmosphere
"And God called the firmament Heaven. And the evening and the morning were the second day"(Genesis 1:8).

The celestial universe
"The heavens declare the glory of God; and the firmament sheweth his handywork" (Psalms 19:1).

The dwelling place of God
"Seeing then that we have a great high priest, that is passed into the heavens, Jesus the Son of God, let us hold fast our profession" (Hebrews 4:14).

In nature, storms are inevitable; just as they are in your life. However, understanding the truth of an eternity beyond this life will help you to refocus. The reality of Heaven prepares you to face whatever storms may come your way.

Life's day will soon be o'er
All storms forever past
We'll cross the great divide to glory safe at last.
We'll share the joys of heaven – a harp, a home, a crown,
The tempter will be banished; we'll lay our burdens down

It will be worth it all when we see Jesus
Life's trials will seem so small when we see Christ.
One glimpse of His dear face all sorrow will erase,
So bravely run the race 'til we see Christ.

Esther Kerr Rusthoi

When our son, Cliff, was told he had cancer and it was growing faster than they first anticipated, I began asking God not to let him die. God answered - not with the answer I had hoped for; but rather He impressed on my mind and my heart these words: "If I truly believed in Heaven, then why would I ask God not to take him there?" It was a sobering thought!

The Promise of Heaven
1. What promise is made in *Titus 1:2?*

This is not an "I hope this happens". It is not wishful thinking; it is based on the reality of God, therefore, a sure thing.

2. This same hope is spoken of in *Hebrews 6:19-20.* How is this hope described?

The function of an anchor is to keep the ship from moving from its position. The anchor cannot be seen, yet it can be depended upon to keep the ship from drifting. God can keep you from drifting away, especially when the winds blow and the waves seem to overtake you.

3. According to *Romans 8:35-39* what can separate you from the Love of God?

4. What promise is made in the following verses?

    John 14:1-3

    Hebrews 9:15

Heaven is a physical place.
5. *Hebrews 11:16* likens Heaven to what?

Heaven is a beautiful place.
6. What kind of picture comes to your mind when you read the following verses?
Luke 23:43

2 Corinthians 12:4

Revelation 2:7

7. Look up "paradise" in the dictionary and write the definition(s) here:

Heaven is a place prepared for believers:
8. In the following verses, who are the recipients of everlasting life?
Matthew 25:46

John 3:16

John 3:36

John 4:14

John 5:24

John 6:40

John 6:47

Romans 6:22, 23

Eternal (everlasting) life does not begin when you die. It begins the moment you make the decision to accept Jesus Christ as your Savior.

9. What does *Revelation 21:1-4* tell you about Heaven?

10. Not only will you, as a believer, live forever in the presence of the Lord, but according to *1 John 3:2* who will you be like?

Heaven is NOT a mental concept. Heaven is real. The perspective of eternity with Christ should make a difference in the way you perceive difficulties, the way you face trials and the way you walk through them.

11. According to *Romans 8:18-25* the sufferings (storms) of this present world should not be compared to what?

12. *Romans 8:25* tells you to what?

13. What is *2 Corinthians 4:17-18* telling you about these afflictions (storms) in your life?

Challenge:
May you bear trials patiently and without complaint in the hope of your future glory, the blessed eternity with your Lord.

Lesson Twelve: Be Not Afraid

The following article was written by Cliff six years into his journey with terminal cancer and one year from his entrance into his Heavenly Home.

One night recently I lay in bed listening to a violent thunderstorm outside. Some of the lightning flashes were very close and lit up the whole bedroom, and the thunder from those flashes would make a loud, sharp CRACK rather than the usual deep rolling boom. It was fabulous! I kept my eyes open as long as I could, not because I was afraid but because I love thunderstorms. Here in New Hampshire we don't get the kind of drenching downpours I grew up with in Florida, but we do sometimes get thunder and lightning that rivals anything I experienced in my childhood.

I enjoy most kinds of extreme weather. I enjoy listening to the wind howling outside a window, and all the better if it's accompanied by a blizzard. I lived in Florida for over 15 years and never was in a hurricane, which to be honest was a great disappointment to me. Fortunately, I did get to experience one several years ago when I went back to visit my parents. Mom and I went outside and stood in the rain and took pictures.

The reason I enjoy thunderstorms, blizzards, and hurricanes is I know that I am safe. My windows are not going to blow out and my roof is not going to cave in. The storm will pass and all will be well. On the other hand, driving in a blizzard or a thunderstorm is a different matter. I don't enjoy that at all, because no matter how careful I am the situation is still inherently dangerous. But safely tucked into my own bed, I am confident that no harm will come to me, and I can listen to a storm rage outside with peace and pleasure. My response to the storm that night reminded me of some deeper spiritual truths. In April my oncologist told me that my cancer had begun growing again. I don't like cancer. Along with cancer comes chemotherapy. I don't like chemotherapy. Along with chemotherapy comes medical bills. I don't like medical bills. In fact, any one of these things is downright scary.´ They are storms that come into my life and upset the singing birds and the clear blue skies.

But a little more thought and prayer made me realize that I have as much reason to be afraid during these storms of life as I do listening to a thunderstorm outside my bedroom window. Don't I have a Savior who has promised never to forsake me (Hebrews 13:5)? Don't I have a Father who has my best interest in mind (Romans 8:32)? Don't I have a God who controls the storm (Colossians 1:16-17)?

In Matthew 8 Jesus' disciples faced a literal storm and they were afraid. The storm must have been incredible, since many of these men had grown up on this very lake, and more than a few sloshing waves would have been required to make them fear for their lives. But fear they did. They were so terrified that they failed to understand the significance of Jesus' sleeping. If they had been calm they surely would have realized that since Jesus was not afraid then they had no reason to be either. But they did take their fears to the right person. They woke Jesus and pleaded with Him to save them. (We may criticize them for their lack of faith, but many of us when faced with a storm just try to handle the whole thing ourselves). When Jesus woke up, He asked them an amazing question: "Why are you afraid?" What a question! They were afraid because of the storm! Anyone could see that. But Jesus' question implied that there was really no reason for them to be afraid. He was in control. He calmed the storm for them, but the disciples were really no safer once the storm was calmed. They certainly felt better, but they had been safe the whole time.

Why am I afraid of cancer, or chemotherapy, or medical bills? Ultimately I am afraid because I don't feel safe. What I need to realize is that I am safe. Jesus is with me during these storms, and He's not wringing his hands wondering what to do. He is in complete control. Sometimes when I pray I think of His question: "Why are you afraid?" The wrong answer is obvious and usually immediate—I am afraid because all these things are happening. But the right answer is just as obvious—because my faith is small, and I'm not thinking about things as they really are.

Once I understand that I am safe, that I am held securely in hands from which no one can snatch me (John 10:28-29), then I understand that there is absolutely no reason to be afraid. I can be at peace, and even enjoy the storm (James 1:2, 4).

My cat doesn't understand storms. While I enjoyed the recent thunderstorm and my wife slept through it, our cat hid under the bed. She was as safe as Megan or me, but she didn't know it and she spent the entire storm hiding and fretting. When we don't have the correct perspective of the storms that come into our lives, we will respond just as improperly, and we will miss the peace and enjoyment that God intends us to have during the storms in our lives.

1. How have these lessons changed your perspective of the storms that come into your life?

2. What steps are you taking to prepare for the storms in your life?

ANSWER KEY

Lesson One: The Approaching Storms

1. *2 Corinthians 4:17*
Paul calls our afflictions (trials – storms) what? **Light**
How long do they last? **For a moment**
What do they result in? **Eternal glory**

2. Although there is a human responsibility for preparing for the storms ahead, without God you are bound to fail.
Philippians 4:13 tells you *through Christ* **I can do all things.**
Philippians 4:19 -- *God will* **supply all your needs** *according to his riches in glory by Christ Jesus.*

3. Write out *1 Peter 5:8-11* in your own words
Pay attention, close attention; Satan is watching and looking for someone to destroy. Resist Him by standing firm in my faith. Understand I am not alone; we all have trials and temptations. But those who know Christ as their savior can look forward to an eternity with Christ. Difficulties are given by God to make me more like Jesus Christ. Give God the glory.

Lesson Two – Building on The Firm Foundation

1. Who is the ONE foundation whose footing is sure?
1 Corinthians 3:11 -- **Jesus Christ**

2. What instructions are given to be anchored to this foundation?
Acts 16:31 -- **Believe on the Lord Jesus Christ**
John 1:12 -- **Receive Him**
Matthew 7:24-27 -- **Hear His Word and act on it (Obey)**

3. What do you need to believe?

Romans 3:23 -- I am a **sinner**

Romans 6:23 -- The payment for my sin is **death**

Isaiah 59:2 -- My sin has **separated** me from God

Ephesians 2:8, 9 -- There is **nothing** I can do to pay for my own sin.

BUT

Romans 5:8 -- Christ **died** for me

1 Peter 3:18; John 14:6 -- That He might **bring me to God and remove the separation I have from God.**

The Bible tells you there is an action you need to take:

Acts 3:19 "**Repent** *ye therefore, and be converted, that your sins may be blotted out, when the times of refreshing shall come from the presence of the Lord.*"

Acts 26:20 " *that they should* **repent** *and* **turn to God.**"

4. Has there been a time in your life when you received Jesus Christ as your personal Savior?
(Write out your testimony here) **Answers will vary**

5. If there has never been a time in your life when you made the decision to accept Jesus Christ as your savior Take action TODAY

Hebrews 3:15 "**Today** *if ye will hear his voice;*"

2 Corinthians 6:2 "**Now** *is the Time to accept Jesus as Savior; Behold, Now is the accepted time; behold,* **now** *is the day of salvation.*"

6. When you receive Him, what will you become?
John 1:12 -- **I will become a child of God.**

7. What comparison is the following verse making in regard to obeying God's Word and disobeying God's Word?
Luke 6:46-49 -- **Obedience is building my life on solid ground where the storms will not destroy me.**

Disobeying is like building on sand which washes away.
8. What do these verses say about this new life?
2 Corinthians 5:17 -- **Old things have passed away.**
Galatians 2:20 -- **As a Christian, my life has changed because Christ is living in me. I am no longer who I was. I am new.**

9. You cannot simply add Christ to your life. Because of who God is, you must make a decision regarding your loyalty toward Him:
Exodus 20:5-6; Exodus 34:14 – *"God is a* **Jealous** *God."*
Matthew 6:24 – *"You cannot serve* **Two Masters."**
Why? **I can only love one. I must love one and hate the other.**

10. The Choice is yours. *Joshua 24:15 "And if it seems evil unto you to serve the Lord,* **choose** *you this day whom ye will serve; whether the gods which your fathers served that were on the other side of the flood, or the gods of the Amorites, in whose land ye dwell: but as for me and my house, we will serve The Lord."*

Lesson Three – Relying on The Water of the Word

1. *John 17:17* – The Word of God is **Truth.**

2. Knowing the Word of God is truth, how can that affect you as you face each day?
Answers may vary: I can depend on His Word for guidance and instruction. I can believe it when it tells me who God is and who I am to God

3. What does *2 Timothy 3:16* tell us about God's Word?
"All scripture is given **by Inspiration** *of God. . .*

-and is profitable
- for **doctrine** *-for* **reproof** *-for* **correction**
-for **instruction in righteousness**"
4. For what purpose is Scripture given?
2 Timothy 3:17 -- **That I, as a child of God can be completely equipped for every good work He has for me. The Word of God will equip me.**

5. The Word of God is necessary for what?
Romans 10:14 -- **must be heard in order to believe**
Romans 10:17 -- **to increase our Faith**

6. According to these verses, what does the Word of God give you?
Psalms 119:129-130 -- **gives me light & understanding**
Psalms 119:104 -- **understanding**
Psalms 119:105 -- **light**

7. List some verses that have helped you specifically during difficult days,
Answers will vary. i.e Isaiah 26:3; Psalms 23

8. How does knowing these verses help you to be prepared for what storms might lie ahead?
Answers will vary; I can rest in Him and His care for me

Lesson Four: Getting to Know God

Know: The Character of God
1. What do these verses tell you regarding the character of God?
Genesis 28:3 -- **God Almighty; all sufficient, mighty one**
Genesis 15:1 -- **He is my shield and protection and our great reward.**

60

Genesis 22:8 -- **He provided the sacrifice. He provides for my needs.**
Exodus 15:26 -- **The one who heals**
Psalms 18:46 -- **The rock; my salvation**
Revelation 19:11 -- **Faithful and true**
Luke 1:37 -- **Nothing is impossible for Him.**

2. What do these verses say about the character of Jesus Christ?
John 10:30 -- **He is the same as God.**
Hebrews 13:8 -- **He is the same yesterday, today and tomorrow; He does not change**.

3. What does this verse tell you about the character of the Holy Spirit?
John 14:16 -- **He is another, just like Jesus Christ; He is the comforter; just like God.**

Know: The Power of God
4. How powerful is your God?
Jeremiah 32:17 -- **He made the heavens and the earth; there is nothing too hard for Him**.
Ephesians 1:19-20 -- **Powerful enough to raised Jesus Christ from the dead.**

5. What do these verses say about God's Power?
Romans 13:1 -- **There is NO power but of God**.
Ephesians 3:20 -- **He is able to do far above anything I might ask or think.**
Jude 1:25 -- **It is for now and forever.**

How can knowing God's power prepare you for the storms ahead?
Ephesians 6:10 -- **His Power will make me strong.**

Know: God is Faithful

6. How does His faithfulness relate to the storms you might face?

Lamentations 3:22 -- **He is always faithful. He is faithful in his mercy toward me; His mercy never ends**

Lesson Five: Getting to Know God More

Know: God is Loving and Kind

1. List His benefits according to *Psalm 103:2-5*

He forgives my sins; heals diseases, he redeemed my life from destruction. Through his death we are recued from an eternity in Hell. He shows lovingkindness to me and tender mercy (holding back from me what I deserve as a sinner). He gives me good things; strengthens me.

Know: God is Wise

2. *Ephesians 1:8* -- **Because I believe God is wise, I can trust Him to be just and fair. The world may be unfair, but God isn't.**

3. Why is Wisdom more precious than anything else you can desire?

Proverbs 3:13-15 -- **What I gain from wisdom is more valuable than material possessions.**

Proverbs 2:10, 20 – **He will direct me to walk in the way that is both true and good; allow me to live a life that is pleasing to God; enable me to see the big picture, keep my cool, form a plan and effectively influence others.**

4. When you know God is wise and He never makes a mistake how can that help you be prepared for the storms ahead?
Answers will vary: We can with confidence place our life in His hands and rest in His care.

Know: Our God is a Sovereign God
5. What did Job recognize even though he could not see?
Job 23:10 -- **When everything is done, he will be better for it. When he is tried he will come forth as gold.**
6. How is God's hand in your life, even when you cannot see?
Romans 8:28-30 -- **I know I belong to Him and when I belong to Him, his purpose is to glorify himself through me; thus in the end I will be glorified.**
Philippians 2:13 -- **God's work in my life is for His pleasure and He makes me desire it also.**
Romans 9:20, 21 -- **His purpose is to make me a vessel of honor. I am the clay, he is the potter.**
Ephesians 2:10 says you are *God's workmanship created* -- **unto good works.**

7. How does this verse relate to the storms that come upon you?
Psalms 84:11-- **God will withhold NO good thing from me. All that He gives me can be called good in His eyes. Even the difficult things in God's eyes are good.**

8. What do these verses say about equipping you?
2 Timothy 2:19-21; 2 Timothy 3:17
As I give myself to be used of God, He will separate me unto himself and I will be prepared for whatever he brings into my life (which he calls good). I can be equipped to handle anything.

9. How does knowing God is in control prepare you for the storms ahead?
Answers may vary: I can rest knowing God is in control and He wants the best for me.

Lesson Six – Recognizing the Holy Spirit

1. *Acts 5:3, 4* -- God and the Holy Spirit are **the same**

2. He possesses all the attributes of deity
1 Corinthians 2:11-12 -- He is all **Knowing**
Psalms 139:7 -- He is **Everywhere**
Job 33:4 -- He has all **Power**
1 John 5:6 -- He possesses **Truth**

The Holy Spirit is Personal
3. When you accept Jesus Christ as your Savior, what does the Holy Spirit of God do?
Romans 8:9 -- **He come to live inside of me.**
1 Corinthians 6:19 -- **My body becomes His temple, and I belong to Him.**
John 14:16 -- **Lives in me forever**

4. What does that make you?
1 Corinthians 3:16; 2 Corinthians 6:16 -- **The temple or sanctuary of the Living God.**

5. What do these verses tell you about the Holy Spirit?
Romans 8:9-11 – **I am sealed which assures me that I belong to Him.**
2 Corinthians 1:22; Ephesians 1:13 – **It is a guarantee He will come and take me with Him. When I have placed my trust in Him, I will one day live with Him in Heaven.**

The Holy Spirit's Purpose
6. What do the following verses tell you about the Holy Spirit's purpose?
John 14:26 -- **To teach me and bring things that I learn to remembrance.**
John 16:13 -- **He will guide me.**
Romans 8:14 -- **He will lead me.**
1 Corinthians 2:9-16 --**Through teaching and helping me to remember the things I learn, He will help me to have the mind of Christ.**

7. How can we go forward with confidence?
John 14:16-18 -- **I know I will not be left alone when the difficulties, trials, and storms come.**

Our responsibility to the Holy Spirit
8. What is your responsibility in regard to the Holy Spirit?
Ephesians 5:1 -- **To be filled with the Holy Spirit . I need to be constantly, moment by moment, controlled by the Holy Spirit.**

9. What are the two warnings given you?
Ephesians 4:30 -- **Do not Grieve the Holy Spirit.**
1 Thessalonians 5:19 -- **Do not Quench; like throwing water on a fire.**

10. *Ephesians 4:31* gives some ways in which you can grieve the Holy Spirit. What are they? **Having bitterness in my life, anger, evil speaking.**

11. How does the Holy Spirit assure you that God is always with you and will never leave you?
Answers will vary. God's Word tells me that I am the temple of the Holy Spirit. The Holy Spirit and God are one, therefore God lives within me.

12. Using two columns, list the evidences of being Spirit Filled from Ephesians and the evidences of letting the Word of Christ dwell in you richly from Colossians.

Be filled with the Spirit	*Let the Word of Christ Dwell in you*
Ephesians 5:18-6:6	*Colossians 3:16-4:5*
Speaking to yourselves in hymns and spiritual songs; singing and making melody in your heart.	**Teaching and admonishing one another in psalms, hymns, and spiritual song.**
Giving Thanks	**Give thanks**
Submitting yourselves one to another	
Wives submit	**Wives submit**
Husbands Love	**Husbands Love**
Children Obey	**Children Obey**
Fathers provoke not	**Fathers provoke not**
Servants obey	**Servants obey**
Masters be fair	**Masters be fair**

13. What do you see?
They are the same: The Evidences of being filled with the Spirit are the same as being in God's Word and allowing it to be the guide for my life.

Lesson Seven – Applying God's Armor

1. Write *James 1:2* in your own words.
Be happy; count it a joyous event when various trials come my way. Saying hail welcome.

2. What does *Ephesians 6:12* tell you about the battle you are fighting?
Our battle is not against flesh and blood; it is against Satan and his demons.

3. Why must you put on the armor?
Ephesians 6:11, 13 -- **It is my only protection to stand against the attacks of Satan.**

4. What qualities and characteristics are you to put on?
Galatians 3:27 -- *For as many of you as have been baptized into Christ have put on* **Christ**.
Romans 13:14-- *But put ye on* **The Lord Jesus Christ** *and make not provision for the flesh, to fulfil the lusts thereof.*
Colossians 3:12 -- *Put on therefore, as the elect of God,* **holy and beloved, bowels of mercies, kindness, humbleness of mind, meekness, longsuffering.**
Ephesians 4:24 -- *And that ye put on the new man,* which after *God is created in* **righteousness** *and true* **holiness**.

The Armor of God
Ephesians 6:14-17
Girdle of **Truth**
Breastplate of **righteousness**
Feet shod with the preparation of the Gospel of **Peace**
Shield of **Faith**
Helmet of **Salvation**
Sword of the **Spirit**

5. What might cause you not to put the whole armor on?
Answers will vary: laziness, reliance on self, doubting God's power, wanting to go my own way.

Our Arsenal

6. According to these verses, what Spiritual resources are available to you?
1 Corinthians 1:30 -- **Wisdom from God, righteousness, sanctification and redemption**
Ephesians 1:7-- **Deliverance from sin and the forgiveness of sin**
Ephesians 1:8 -- **Wisdom and prudence -understanding**
Hebrews 4:16 -- **Grace and Mercy**
Romans 5:5 -- **Love**

7. When sin comes knocking at your door, you DO NOT have to answer.
However, when you do sin God is faithful and just to . . .
1 John 1:9 -- **He forgives me and cleanses me from all unrighteousness. Makes me clean again.**

Lesson Eight – The Promises of God

1. Write in your own words the promises given to the Israelites:
Deuteronomy 33:25 -- **God will provide the strength I need for each day.**
Isaiah 40:31-- **The Lord will renew my strength as I wait on Him.**
Psalms 50:15 -- **God will deliver me when I call on Him. He is ready to hear me and deliver me.**
Jeremiah 29:12 -- **God will hear me.**
Psalms 91:15 -- **God will be with me in trouble. He will deliver me. He will honor me.**

Gen 28:15 -- **God will not leave his children and He will fulfill His promises.**
Deuteronomy 33:27 -- **God is my refuge. Satan, the believer's enemy, will be destroyed.**
Joshua 1:9 -- **God is with me at all times, everywhere I go.**
Psalms 27:1-- **The Lord is my strength because He is my salvation – I do not need to be afraid.**
Psalms 138:7-8 -- **God will revive me when I need the strength when Satan attacks me with doubt and fear. God will make perfect whatever I face.**
Psalms 46:1-11 -- **The Lord is my refuge and strength, a very present help in trouble. He is powerful and wants us to behold Him and be still as He is exalted.**

2. Who is the seed? *Genesis 17:7* and *Galatians 3:16*
The coming Messiah – Jesus Christ

3. According to the following verses who is the great promise of the New Testament?
Acts 2:33; Luke 11:13; Luke 24:49 -- **The Holy Spirit**

4. At the time of salvation, a believer is promised the presence of the Holy Spirit as helper, tutor and guide. How long does the presence of the Holy Spirit last?
John 14:16 -- **He will abide with me forever.**

5. What does *2 Corinthians 1:20-22* tell us about the promises of God? **They are all mine!**

6. In *2 Peter 1:3-4,* Peter submits to the Gentiles that God had also given them promises. What are some of them?
Great and Precious: All things that pertain to life and godliness; whatever I need to live a victorious Christian life has been given to me. We are partakers of the divine nature: and Through Christ we have

escaped the corruption of the world; yet I live each day dependent on Him in order to live like who I am in Christ.

7. Because of your relationship with Christ, make a personal application to these promises?

John 14:13 -- **Ask and He will answer so He can be glorified.**

Colossians 2:10 -- **take courage; I have all I need in Him to defeat Satan.**

Romans 8:37-39 -- **I am more than a conqueror. Nothing can separate me from the Love of God. I am the victor.**

1 John 4:4 -- **I can overcome the temptation of Satan for God is stronger. Satan can do nothing to me that God cannot enable me to overcome.**

1 John 5:4-5 -- **Those who are born again can overcome what the world throws at them. My faith is the victory because I have believed in Christ.**

1 Corinthians 15:57 -- **Through Jesus Christ, I have the victory – Satan was defeated; now I do not have to come under Satan's power. The battle has been won.**

Romans 8:31 -- **If God be for me– who can be against me – who can win against God? God and I are the majority.**

Philippians 1:6 -- **God will finish the work He has begun in me since before I was born and continues until I stand before Him face to face.**

Philippians 4:7 -- **God's peace is available and will keep my mind and heart on Him. It is a peace that the unsaved cannot understand and sometimes I don't understand it.**

Hebrews 13:5 -- **Jesus Christ will never, no never, no never, no never, no never leave me or forsake me. The Spirit of Christ dwells inside of me.**

Matthew 7:7-8 -- **God will not hide from me. If I seek Him, He is there. If I call on Him – He will answer.** *John 6:35* -- **When I go to God, He will provide all I need spiritually to live healthy in this life.**

8. It is important to note while the promises of God are afforded to all believers, they do carry a few stipulations. What are the stipulations given to the Israelites in *2 Chronicles 7:14* and how can you apply it to yourself? **I need to humble myself (not be prideful), call upon God (total reliance on Him), seek God's Will (not doing what we want) and turn from sin to God, starting with salvation and continuing through my life in the way I live.**

9. In *John 15:4-10,* what is the stipulation given to believers? **Abide in Him. Keep His commandments, live by faith**

10. *Lamentations 3:22-25 "It is of the LORD's mercies that we are not consumed, because his compassions fail not. They are new every morning: great is thy faithfulness. The LORD is my portion, saith my soul; therefore will I hope in him. The LORD is good unto them that* **wait** *for him, to the soul that* **seeketh** *him."*

11. If God says; no good thing will he withhold from them who walk uprightly - then how should you view the storms in your life? **As good; they are profitable events in the eyes of God, therefore I should view them as the same.**

12. How can you keep your mind stayed on Jesus Christ? **By being in the Word of God and focusing on who He is, not on the circumstances I find myself in.**

Lesson Nine – Standing on Praying Ground

1. What would cause you to become disconnected?
Psalms 66:17-20 -- **Holding onto sin in my heart.**
Isaiah 59:2 -- **Sin**

2. What does *Psalms 34:15* and *Proverbs 15:29* tell you about God hearing?
He hears the cries of the righteous.

3. *John 9:31* tells us God does not have to hear **sinners** but God does hear **worshippers of God.**

4. What do these verses say about prayer?
1 Peter 4:7 -- **The end of my life is at hand so be serious about prayer. Take every opportunity to pray.**
Colossians 4:2 -- **Continue in prayer – maintain the spirit of prayer - I must be in the right frame of mind to pray.**
Luke 18:1 -- **Take every opportunity to pray; keep praying even when I do not see answers.**
Philippians 4:6 -- **Pray in time of need. Give it to God. God already knows what I need, but He wants me to ask anyway. He wants that personal communication.**
Ephesians 6:18 -- **I am in a spiritual battle. I must go forward in prayer. It is one of the greatest weapons I have in the battle.**

5. The following verses say about commitment to prayer?
Psalm 102:2 – "*Hide not thy face from me in the day when I am in trouble;* **incline your ear toward me**: *in the day when I call answer me speedily.*"
Psalm 88:1-2 "*O LORD God of my salvation, I have* **cried day and night** *before thee: Let my prayer come before thee:* **incline thy ear** *unto my cry.*"
Nehemiah 1:6 "*Let thine ear now be* **attentive**, *and thine eyes open, that thou* **may hear the prayer** *of thy servant.*"

6. What is God's promise to His children who are committed to prayer?
John 14:13-14 -- **God does hear and will answer. His answer will be to bring glory to Himself.**
Matthew 6:5-8 – **God knows all things: He will reward those who pray to Him**

7. What are some conditions given for prayer?
1 John 3:22-- keep **his commandments, and do those things that are pleasing in his sight**
1 John 5:14-- **if we ask any thing according to his will**
Mark 11:24-- when ye pray, **believe that ye receive them,**
8. What promises are given in these verses regarding prayer?
Jeremiah 33:3 -- **God says "Pray and I will answer". His answer will be great and mighty.**
Ephesians 3:20 -- **God can do great things far above what I ask or even think. According to His Power – WOW - His Power, not my own.**
Galatians 6:6 -- **God teaches all good things.**

9. What was the result of Jesus' prayer in *Luke 22:42-46*?
Jesus human nature was hurting. His prayer was for God's Will to be done. God strengthened him.

Lesson Ten – Faithfulness in the Local Church

1. *Matthew 16:18*
Who builds the church? **God builds the church.**
How strong is the church? **Satan cannot defeat it.**

2. *Acts 20:28*
With whose blood was it purchased? **Jesus Christ**

3. Paul is comparing the body of Christ to what?
Ephesians 5:30 -- **The human body**

1 Corinthians 12:12-13 -- **The human body**

4. Fill in the blank to see what God expects of the church regarding unity.
Romans 12:4-5 "For as we have many members in **one** *body, and all members have not the same office: So we, being many, are* **one** *body in Christ, and every* **one** *members* **one** *of another."*
Ephesians 4:4 "There is **one** *body, and one Spirit, even as ye are called in* **one** *hope of your calling;"*

5. *Act 2:41-42*
Who makes up the local church? **Those who are saved and have been baptized.**

What are the main activities of the local church? **The teaching of the Word of God, fellowship with one another, communion and prayers.**

6. *Ephesians 4:12*
What is the purpose of the local church? **For fellowship, the teaching of God's Word, and equipping the saints so they can carry out God's work.**

7. *Acts 6:1-4*
The Twelve had two major responsibilities: **Prayer and the teaching of the Word.**
Meeting the physical needs of the believers was also important. What do these verses tell you regarding how they met those needs? **They chose 12 men to serve the needs of the people.**

8. Meditate on *Ephesians 4:16.* Write it in your own words
It takes the whole body working together; each one giving their gifts and talents so that the church is an effective ministry and each one within the church is

74

growing and bringing unity and strengthened by the
love they have for one another.

9. What instructions is God giving to the believers within the
Universal Church as well as the believers in the local church?
Ephesians 4:32 -- **Be kind to one another, be forgiving.**
Colossians 3:13-16 -- **Be patient with one another,
forgive one another. Have love toward one another,
walk close with God and keep in His Word so that our
lives will reflect Him.**
Romans 13:8 -- **Love one another – owe man nothing –
do not be indebted to another: be honest in our
dealings with one another.**

John 13:34 -- **Love one another – the way Christ loves –
forgiving, uplifting and seeking the good of the other.**
1 Peter 4:10 -- **Minister to one another; benefit the
other person by meeting their needs through the
talents and gifts God has given you.**
Galatians 6:2 -- **Bear one another's burdens;
encourage, lift up, pray for.**

9. According to *Hebrews 10:24, 25* what instruction is given
you concerning the local church?
**When the writer of Hebrews tells the believers to
consider one another to love and to good works he
wants them to put some effort into it bringing unity
and strength so they can hold fast to what they had
been taught.**

Lesson Eleven – Looking Toward Heaven

The Promise

1. What promise is made in *Titus 1:2*? **The hope of Eternal life**

2. This same hope is spoken of in *Hebrews 6:19-20*. How is this hope described? **As an anchor. Sure and steadfast.**

3. According to *Romans 8:35-39* what can separate us from the Love of God? **Nothing; absolutely nothing**

4. What promise is made in the following verses?
John 14:1-3 -- **A mansion is being prepared for me as a believer in Jesus Christ and Jesus is coming again to take me into heaven.**
Hebrews 9:15 -- **An eternal inheritance is for those who have been redeemed (saved). Jesus paid my debt.**

Heaven is a physical place.

5. *Hebrews 11:16* likens Heaven to what?
A better country; heavenly – a city.

Heaven is a beautiful place:

6. What kind of picture comes to your mind when you read the following verses?
Luke 23:43, 2 Corinthians 12:4, Revelation 2:7
Paradise; beautiful, restful, enjoyable

7. Look up "Paradise" in the dictionary and write the definition(s) here:
Bliss, utopia, a place or state of perfect happiness Heaven, a Place ideally suited to somebody. Where there is everything that a particular person needs for his or her interest.

Heaven is a place prepared for believers:

8. In the following verses, who are the recipients of everlasting life?
Matthew 25:46 – **Those who are righteous.**
John 3:16 -- **Whosoever believes in Jesus Christ.**
John 3:36 -- **He that believes in Jesus Christ.**
John 4:14 -- **Whoever drinks of the living Water/ Acceptance of Jesus Christ**
John 5:24 -- **He who hears the Word and believes in God: hearing, understanding and obeying. Faith in both the one who sent and the one who is sent.**
John 6:40 -- **Those who believes in Jesus.**
John 6:47 -- **Believes on Jesus Christ.**
Romans 6:22, 23 -- **One who has been freed from sin because they have received the free gift of salvation.**

9. What does *Revelations 21:1-4* tell us about Heaven?
It is a place without sorrow, darkness or any kind of sin.

10. Not only will you, as a believer, live forever in the presence of the Lord, but according to *1 John 3:2* what will you be like? **I will be like Christ.**

11. The sufferings (storms) of this present world should not be compared to what?
Romans 8:18 -- **The glorious hope for the future – what will be revealed to me in Heaven.**

12. *Romans 8:25* tells us to what? **Wait patiently for it.**

13. What is *2 Corinthians 4:17-18* telling you about these afflictions (storms) in your life?
They are light and they are for a moment.

The storms will produce in us a greater weight of glory; I will look to God and see Him glorified through the storms.

Lesson Twelve: Be Not Afraid

1. How have these lessons changed your perspective of the storms that come into your life?

Answers will vary

2. What steps have you taken to prepare for the storms in your life?

Answers will vary:

12363360R00044

Made in the USA
Middletown, DE
23 November 2018